response

poems by

Patricia J. Boyle

Finishing Line Press
Georgetown, Kentucky

response

ACKNOWLEDGMENTS

Grateful acknowledgment is made to the following publications in which
these poems or earlier versions first appeared (sometimes with different
titles):

California Writers Club Tri-Valley Branch Anthology, *Voices of the Valley:
Word for Word*, 2015: "Saturday Morning Encounter," "Wild Geese on a Gray
Morning"
California Writers Club *Literary Review*, 2016: "Saturday Morning
Encounter"
Las Positas College Anthology *Beyond the Window*, 2017: "First Storm of the
Season"
California Writers Club Tri-Valley Branch Anthology, *Voices of the Valley:
Through the Window*, 2020: "Aurora"
Las Positas College Anthology, *Havik: We Are Here*, 2022: "Observations of a
Silent Bystander"
Summertime Fireflies, (Wingless Dreamer), 2022: "Apple Tree Roost"
Las Positas College Anthology, *Havik: Cacophony*, 2023: "Musings Amidst a
Drought," "Mutual Regard," "soap bubble"

Publisher: Leah Huete de Maines
Editor: Christen Kincaid
Cover Art: Patricia Boyle
Author Photo: Kerry Boyle
Cover Design: Elizabeth Maines McCleavy

Order online: www.finishinglinepress.com
also available on amazon.com

Author inquiries and mail orders:
Finishing Line Press
PO Box 1626
Georgetown, Kentucky 40324
USA

Contents

For Jim

First Night

Tail end of August. Mild air, a quarter moon
smiled benignly. Stars glittered, mirroring
our nervous excitement. In the distance,
beyond the town, stretched the beckoning finger
of the deep glacial lake.

We sat on a grassy slope that joined the dorm
complex below with the arts quad above. Suspended
in time, a handful of us, newly met, talked
the way strangers do. Superficial conversation.
Where are you from? What's your major?
The words didn't really matter.

We sat on the edge of the future. Our futures.
In afternoon farewells to families, we released
our pasts, or at least loosened our grip. Soon,
reality would come for us. But this night, for
a few hours, the magic of the unknown held sway.

We sat together past midnight, sipping cartons
of chocolate milk. Palavering, laughing, drunk on
the elixir of limitless possibility floating on the breeze.

Impressions in Wax

Jasmine, vanilla, mahogany, bamboo.
I sort through fragrant waxen rolls.
Lavender, cedar, cardamom, and oud.
Choosing one that suits my frame
of mind, I strike a match, watch a flame
flare into life, settle with a book
in my favorite chair.

The dog walks by—smelly, in need
of a bath. It's too cold now, we'll bear
her odor till the next warm spell.
My thoughts tumble back through
the centuries—to the eighteenth,
sixteenth, fifteenth, twelfth—when
animals slept at one end of a dwelling,
humans at the other.

I picture my rustic ancestors,
jammed together with aromatic
sheep and cows all winter long,
sharing the scanty warmth of a smoky
cook fire. Pungent tallow candles poured
dim light over bowls of meaty stew
and thick slices of chewy bread.

I gaze at the dancing candle flame,
seeking ancient family. What habits
of mine did they share? Which traits
of theirs do I carry?

Unidirectional Flow

Thin stream of burbling water responds
to gravity's pull, tumbles downward,
ever downward, weaves with dancing
mountainous flows. Growing wider, deeper,
rushing white-foamed over sandy bottom,
stirs and churns loose particles, transforming
sparkling, clear water into a muddy ocher matrix
bearing tangled branches and debris.

Downstream, coursing placidly, wavelets
curve, embrace weathered humps of rock,
lap the shore of midstream
islands, ripple over quiet pools
where fish linger in the shade
and leaves collect in multi-colored
heaps, nestled between soggy
roots of overhanging trees.

Meandering, eroding,
incrementally altering the landscape,
a ribbon of wide, lazy loops
caresses Earth's flat bosom and slowly,
slowly, spreads glimmering, thin fingers
across a fan-shaped delta. Weary, tranquil,
released from confinement, the river's fresh waters
swirl into the welcoming current of a vast, briny sea.

Fog of Unreality

A mist drifts lazily across
the back garden.

It spreads a thin veil
over the flower bed,
muting colors,
softening edges.

A thick gray blanket forms
by the vegetable patch,
obscuring familiar features.

A curtain hangs
in the center of the yard.
Tiny silvery spheres
gleam in the pale, creamy
light of the rising sun.

I pass by the window
and pause, transfixed
by the shifting cloud,
my morning routine
forgotten.

Ah, the slyness of water.

Wild Geese on a Gray Morning

The geese fly low overhead, calling
to each other with trumpeting blasts.
They flap in rhythm, heading east
in ragged formation, two lagging behind.

The still air feels damp and cool on my skin.
A thick sheet of cloud hides the sun.
Void of color, the honking silhouettes
rise and fall beneath the ashen sky.

I gaze at their retreating forms, held in
place by undulating motion and lonely cries.
The melancholy sound sinks into my bones.
In silent communion, I yearn to fly.

Keeping Watch

Brandy sits by the window
alone. An ebony statuette
adorned in Grecian curls.
Quiet, but for a mournful
whine when someone passes by.

After a time, she vacates
her seat to roam
from room to room,
hunting without success
for her absent mistress.

I am the only one present—
an inferior understudy.
Padding past me on silent paws,
she settles onto her perch
on the sofa to resume her vigil.

Gazing, waiting, breaking my heart.

Saturday Morning Encounter

Banking complete, I cross
the empty parking lot. A small
movement catches my eye,
slows my steps. Silent as mist,
a young man rises behind
a dumpster, stretching muscles
stiffened by asphalt. A sleeping bag,
cocoon against the night's chill,
dangles from his hands.

Auburn hair tousled,
dark coat faded and stained,
he stands tall and straight
in the morning sun.

We glance at each other,
a fleeting connection. Unwilling
witness to a stranger's awakening,
I tread lightly past his private space.
Gaze averted, he rolls his bag
with slow, steady movements.
I open my car and slip inside,
sending one last look his way.

When I return months later,
his spot's unoccupied.
But the stately youth
in ancient clothes lingers
in my mind.

Mutual Regard

We met on the path
by the gym, my workout
clothes stuffed in a bag
slung over my shoulder.
The bright-eyed forager
scampered toward a tree,
bushy tail held high, gripping
a seed between padded paws.

We paused our steps,
viewed each other
in silence for a moment.
Discerning no threat,
we parted ways
with a nod of a head
and a twitch of a tail,
each to our own pursuit.

Observations of a Silent Bystander

The chatter of children at morning recess
bounces over the fence top—bright bursts
of laughter, high-pitched fragments of excited
exchanges, and free-floating shrieks of joy.

Afternoon is filled with birdsong—
light chirpings and sweet, clear
melodies. The notes fall from above
like the patter of raindrops.

By evening the twitter of birds gives way
to frog song—a bubbling soprano chorus
of puffy-throated peepers searching for a mate.
Such a private ritual to be carried on the air.

I do not see the beings who commune, nor
understand the whole of what they're saying,
yet my heart grows lighter, sorrows lessen,
when I overhear their vibrant conversations.

Musings Amidst a Drought

Sunshine floods the field,
bathing wildflowers
and weeds in amber light.
Golden days follow one another
across the forecast calendar
like a row of fuzzy ducklings.

Rain is a distant memory.

Nascent clouds evaporate, revealing
skies of blinding blue. Skin bakes
and flakes in hot, moisture-hungry
air. Steering wheels and seats
scorch unprotected limbs.

Thirsty as the soil, I await thick
dark clouds and fat raindrops
splashing onto sidewalks,
dripping off branches, rushing
into drains clogged with dusty leaves
and discarded fast-food wrappers.

A Natural Occurrence

The storm this weekend
brought a steady, soaking rain.

Water trickled
into the earth,
filling the interstices
between particles of soil,
to be absorbed by tiny
root hairs of trees,
bushes, flowers,
and weeds.

There were few accidents
on the roadways,
minimal flooding,
no burst dams.

The media was,
understandably,
disappointed.

manhattan oasis

heat flows off city sidewalks in waves
i am drowning in a shuffling
river of perspiring souls
a diminutive park
proffers a lifeline
water ripples
over rock
be still
be

response

sometimes conditions are just right—
the sky a picture book
robin's egg blue with clouds
that stretch like cotton candy
from the county fair,
the cool breeze reminiscent
of the best spring days of childhood—
I begin to think the day
can't be improved

then my attention is caught
by bobbing flowers on a lone tree
in a circle of grass, its blossoms
the palest pink with fuchsia veins,
delicate ruffles of such loveliness
they make my chest ache

the only worthy response
I can offer is a period
of profound silence

First Storm of the Season

Outside, thick
pewter clouds hurl
rain at the windows in
slanted sheets, as the wind
twirls leafy branches in a dance.

I read while the dog sleeps,
deaf to the neighbor's rhythmic
drumbeat seeping through the walls.

The storm
blows itself out.
A weary sun blesses
the cloud tops, sculpting
heaps of candescent confections.

I stand beside the glistening
apple tree. A shaft of sunlight warms
my face, cool air caresses outstretched limbs.

Rain-dappled ginger beckons
from the garden. Blazing tangerine,
awash with miniature, reflective worlds.

the day after

yesterday the vet
uttered the words
enlarged spleen
swollen lymph nodes
lymphoma
in hushed tones

the terms
explained so much—
your decreased appetite
unsteady gait
taking refuge under
the ottoman
as if in a cave

you looked at us
with complete trust
and we understood
it was time
so we let you go

today I am
thirty-six thousand
feet in the air
my heart
a lump of lead
that fills my chest
so heavy,
it's a wonder
the weight of it
doesn't pull
the plane
down

Apple Tree Roost

Rough bark scrapes against my shin
as I climb to my perch and settle in
between knobby, angled branches.
Leafy emerald curtains shield
me from the outside world.

The lawn slants down and away,
then flattens out, spreading
its narrow blades generously
to the edge of Dad's carefully
tended vegetable garden.

Mom's flower bed brims over
with spotted orange tiger lilies
and their lemon-yellow cousins.

Behind the rhubarb patch
is the spot where I knelt
on a squashy toad in the dark
during a neighborhood game
of hide-and-seek.

In winter, we sledded
down the gentle slope
beneath me and skated
on a homemade rink—
a pitted slab of ice
beside the hibernating
mound of lilies.

Adjusting my position,
I breathe in the heady scent
of lilac wafting on the breeze.

I sit alone with my book,
alone with my thoughts,
quietly, contentedly,
                        alone.

Summertime Happening

Hour by hour, the clouds grow thicker,
billowing in the hot afternoon. Puffy
gray towers swell overhead
then level out, flat anvils
miles above the earth.

Inhaling the clean scent of ozone,
I rush to take the laundry off
the line. Clothespins dropped
by ones and twos plink against
the sides of a battered can,
counterpoint to the tinny notes
from my transistor radio.

The afternoon light
takes on a dusky hue.
Rising wind and distant rumbling
proclaim an imminent disturbance.

Sharp blades of lightning slice
the sticky air. Cracks of thunder
chase the flashes, arriving quicker
and quicker after each brilliant streak.

I watch the ensuing deluge
with my father, from the doorway
of the attached garage. My mother
sits upon the sofa, praying over
glossy rosary beads.

Sooner than I wish, the raw
power of the storm gives way
to golden silence. Wisps of steam
ascend between puddles scattered
over blacktop, while droplets
clear as rain-washed air
cling resolutely to the peonies.

soap bubble

buoyant, shimmering sphere
ephemeral ball of beauty

soft and wet, yet strong enough
to hold a swirling rainbow

floating, drifting on currents of air,
you're a dancing child, joyous and light

fairy fine, yet releasing a tear
i reach out a hand to guide you

you follow my lead,
but your message is clear—

*i'll let you come close
and accept your affection,*

*though i'm not part of you,
and don't want your protection*

*you may share in my life,
yet don't hold me too tight,*

*for if you constrict me,
i'll wink out of sight*

mirage

a slender stem
with ends entwined
winds round my finger
gleams in the light

smooth silver leaves
dainty and neat
its path to formation
didn't start in a seed

mined from the earth
then refined and shaped
in an exquisite form
containing much charm

yet not a true vine—
this lustrous circlet
never will grow
never will know

the uptake of water
the intake of air
the spark of creation
the cycle of life

Aurora

By nature's hand, light spreads across the sky,
a waving flag of undulating light.
Bright swirls of color glow and dance on high,
to awe the soul that watches in the night.

A fearsome storm of mighty energy,
of plasma hurled away from distant sun.
Across the miles it streams, but we can't see,
till atmospheric fireworks have begun.

Then radio's clear signal may be gone,
and satellites don't function as before.
Yet Roman goddess of the glowing dawn,
bedazzles and compels us to adore.

Thick air that lies between the earth and space,
provides protection to us all with grace.

Conus marmoreus

the marbled shell fits
comfortably in my hand
it feels cool and smooth
i rub my thumb over
the glossy surface
and imagine the living snail
rippling across the sandy
sea floor on its muscular foot

ivory triangles adorn the exterior—
rows of sunbathers in assorted sizes
lazing on a beach of dark sand,
each robed in a thin orange band

the pattern suggests wrapping paper
a cone-shaped present topped
with an elegant spiral

but this is no gift—

> *The poison combines hundreds*
> *of toxins, blocking efforts to produce*
> *antivenom. Victims may suffer*
> *pain, numbness, and fatal paralysis.*

hidden in a coral reef
the speckled creature lies in wait
when prey comes near, it shoots its harpoon—
                              delivering death in a jab

Flowering Dogwood

Your branches spread
far in all directions,
curving outward,
upward, in graceful
arcs that taper down
to slender tips.

Showy white flowers
adorn your crown
In a brilliant blaze
of glory that pulls
my gaze from every
tree around you.
They hold fast
against lashing rain
and steady wind.

Your width is much greater
than your height.
It took decades
for you to grow
this fine.

Never mind your blossoms
are not true flowers.
Forget the confusion
over how your name
came to be. Ignore
the patchy lichen
covering your bark.

You be you, dogwood.
Grow older with confidence,
spread your limbs, bloom
as long as you wish, be
the beauty your seedling
self was destined to be.

Rhododendron

At first you appeared
monolithic, brooding
in your deep green garb,
sheltering in the shade
of the house, quietly
keeping to yourself.

I bided my time, asked
nothing of you, silently
sharing the view
of wooded grounds.
As the days went by
you softened, until
ready to present
your hidden beauty.

Formal green gave way
to brilliant colors.
Rolled magenta bundles
split open ivory buds.
Delicate rosy stars unfurled,
laced with yellow bars,
while hot pink stamens
curved like beckoning
fingers, luring bees to coat
themselves in pollen.

Imagine if I'd picked
a different time of year
to visit. In early spring
you'd only show your
somber side. Your blooms
will fade by autumn's
frosty days, and winter
snows will hide your bulk
from view.

Consider if I'd hurried home,
and hadn't allowed time
for you to open up.

With poorer timing, I would
have missed your splendor,
only met a portion of the real you.

Spring in the Wildflower Patch

a pink poppy grows
  by the birdbath
    its petals thin slices of sunrise

pale, narrow leaves
  grace the tender
    green stem that sways
      in response to a caressing breeze

a harbinger, this fluttering beacon
  of a multi-colored, soft
    carpet of blooms

birds flit in and out
  of the freshly awakened garden
    cool water slips down
      tiny throats

beaks nip at scattered seed
  while toes dig lightly
    into crumbly
      dark soil

evening walk

we stood on the curve of the Earth
and gazed at the western sky

where the moon shone white
with light borrowed from the Sun

over its shoulder hung Jupiter
glowing brighter than any star

the neighborhood was quiet
the air still and cool

a smile lit your face
and took away the chill

then we and the dog
ambled down the street

pausing while she sniffed
at every bush along the way

Patricia J. Boyle is a San Francisco Bay Area writer, born and raised in upstate New York. She has fond memories of spring-blooming forsythia, summer Adirondack camping trips, colorful fall foliage, and cold, snowy winters. She inherited a belief in possibilities from her father and a love of poetry from her mother, with Edgar Allan Poe, Carl Sandburg, and Robert Frost early favorites.

She earned a B.S. in earth science and math education from Cornell University and an M.S. in atmospheric science from SUNY Albany. After teaching in northeastern colleges for a few years, she moved with her husband to California, where they have remained ever since. She was a research meteorologist in Monterey and later taught in the Livermore school district until retirement.

Patricia's writing has focused on poetry, a young adult fantasy novel, short stories, and news articles for a local symphony. She draws inspiration from the natural world and human nature. Her writing has appeared in many anthologies, including the California Writers Club *Literary Review, Havik, Voices of the Valley*, and Wingless Dreamer publications. Her work has won awards from *Wow! Women on Writing, Writer's Digest*, and Bay Area organizations. Patricia is past president of the Tri-Valley Branch of the California Writers Club and author of *Traitor in the Realm*. This is her first chapbook. Visit her at *www.patriciajboyle.co*m and at *https://www.facebook.com/ PatricaJBoyle*

www.ingramcontent.com/pod-product-compliance
Lightning Source LLC
Chambersburg PA
CBHW022101080426
42734CB00009B/1441